Full of Life

SEAN PATRICK MILLER

ISBN: 1534808345
ISBN-13: 9781534808348

DEDICATION

To the three Mothers who have always been in my life

Firstly, I offer this book up to Our Mother of Perpetual Help, who has always guided and protected me throughout the course of my life.

Secondly, I remember my loving Mother, June Miller, who taught me the true meaning of patience and empathy by showing me the importance of being a sympathetic listener. Your "Silent Strength" is always with me!

Thirdly, to my dearest Godmother and sister, Theresa. Your tender way of loving everyone who you come in contact with is an unwavering testimony to what "Unconditional Love" really means.

CONTENTS

ACKNOWLEDGMENT

A very special thanks to Liz O'Brien who helped all throughout the making of this book. Thank you for your editing, rearranging and priceless suggestions. Honestly, this book would have never come to fruition without your guidance and help. Thank you a million times, Liz!

1 A FOUNDATION OF LIES

If somebody wants you to do something and they sense resistance on your part, it is not uncommon for them to use manipulation. Manipulation is another way to "bend the truth," so that it works in one's favor. It is more commonly known as lying. This is the foundation upon which the entire abortion industry is founded.

The industry uses a number of tactics in order to persuade women to have abortions. One tactic is the "choice" mentality. They tell women they should not have their freedom to choose taken away from them. They tell them, "This is your right! You should be able to do what you want with your body."

The problem with this mentality is that the choice that women are being offered will ultimately hurt them on many levels — not to mention their own baby's life is being taken.

Nowadays, people mistake freedom to mean that you can do whatever you want regardless of how it affects others. As long as it makes you happy ... just do it! Nobody has a right to do what is evil. Here the abortion industry offers a service to supposedly help women. Yet these women are left all alone to suffer once the abortion is performed. The industry made their money and that is the bottom line. Now women have been lied to by the use of the "freedom" slogan when, in reality, they have lost their freedom psychologically as they now are burdened with the guilt of abortion. It is not until they decide to come to God for forgiveness and healing that they can truly regain that freedom once again.

Another tactic abortion supporters like to use is the "fear tactic." The fear tactic is closely linked with a preoccupation with self. This preoccupation points to the inconveniences this child will bring.

Here are some of the common objections: I am still in school ... what about my education and career? What will my family say? I am not ready to be a mother! I am too young to be a mother ... I want to live my life! What if my baby has a disability?

All of these objections take the concern for the baby and invert it towards the mother, to the point that the mother feels inconvenienced and perhaps embarrassed about her pregnancy.

However, this shows little or no concern for the baby at all. Yes, it is true that the mother could very well be in a difficult situation, but the reality is that she is presently a mother. Now sacrifices will have to be made because an infant who is completely helpless and dependent needs help. All of these fear tactics point to the desires of the mother, without any regard to the needs of the baby. In short, selfishness needs to be replaced by selflessness.

Similar to the fear tactic is the "despair tactic." The industry despises prolife pregnancy centers. If they sincerely cared about their clients, they would openly make them aware of the many other alternatives that are available. Instead, they like to be perceived as the "gallant knight" that will willingly save the woman in despair from her present plight. In so doing, they hurt and exploit women in their hour of greatest need. This is all done for their "idol," which is the dollar.

Ironically, these abortionists that somehow call themselves doctors go against the very nature of their profession. The "calling" of doctors and nurses is a call to service, which promotes and brings about healing in order to sustain life. The abortion industry does none of this. Worse than that, the industry hurts the vulnerable and destroys the innocent.

These three main tactics: choice, fear, and despair are the bedrock of the abortion industry. Couples are exploited to think that they have no other choice but to abort their child. The prolife movement wishes to let couples know that there is always hope. This hope continues to grow as year by year more and more pregnancy centers come into existence. Prolife groups are growing internationally as they only seek to help couples and show them the beauty of "life."

It is also very important that we expose the lies of the abortion industry, and we must do this by educating others, most especially the youth. By doing this, women will learn about the reality of the life of the baby in the womb, and veils of fear and despair can also be lifted. They will be lifted because the vast numbers of organizations and people that want to help will be revealed. Unlike the abortion industry, the prolife groups sincerely care about the health and lives of both the mother and the baby. The prolife foundation is one that is built on truth and hope.

Let us light the torch of hope as we go forward to tell the truth about The Miracle of Life!

2 MARCH FOR LIFE 2013
VERY MUCH ALIVE

On a bitterly cold January morning a group of 31 people boarded a bus to embark on a journey that would unite them with over 500,000 people. This daylong journey would lead us to our nation's capital. Every year at this time, hundreds of thousands of Americans unite at this destination to celebrate the gift of life. This celebration is marred with the unfortunate legalization of abortion, which took place 40 years ago.

On this day, we urge the people in power to respect the sanctity of life. We pray that their hardened hearts open up so that they can be open to the gift of life, in particular, a life that is innocent, defenseless and most vulnerable. In our nation, which is known for being the land of the free, we have discriminated against those who are powerless and cannot defend themselves. Perhaps, since they have no voice it is easier to do so. Well, on this day we stand in solidarity with one powerful voice pleading for the unborn who only ask for the "right to life." How can a country turn its back on a completely dependent little baby? Since when is it inconvenient to care for those who are most in need? If this is the case, then we truly are a poor nation. Our own selfish desires have filled our hearts with greed to the point that we have no room to care for an innocent little baby.

The fact that people attempt to justify such killings shows how clouded our thinking has become. A country that was founded on generations of selfless acts has now become a country filled with "selfish attacks." That is right -- attacks! The womb is known as a place for warmth, growth, and nourishment. It has become a battlefield of brutal attacks on life. When a home is burglarized the homeowners feel violated in an indescribable manner. The home of the womb is violated as the little soul that is seeking only care is unexpectedly taken from his home -- from his existence. Why is this acceptable?

When this occurs 4,000 times on a daily basis in the United States of America, how can we stand by silently? Another disturbing reality is that many Americans remain indifferent to this tragedy. When you discuss the abortion issue with many people they have the attitude that it does not directly affect them so why should they get involved? They might say, "I think abortion is horrible and I would never have one but I am not going to tell anybody else what to do." If you agree that it is horrible than why would it be okay for someone else to do it? Would you say the same thing about an elderly woman whom you witnessed being beaten and robbed? How could you walk away with an indifferent attitude? If you did you would share in the guilt of the crime by a serious sin of omission.

Did God put us on this earth so that we live in our own "personal bubbles," with tunnel vision? Are we called to just "mind our own business?" Are we just like cells that bounce off one another without any sense of responsibility for each other? I would like to think that the opposite is true. When we see someone in trouble it ought to be our moral obligation to help them. At least, we should offer the help even if it is not accepted. The worst-case scenario for anybody is to feel that there is no help available and they are left all alone.

The couple that finds themselves in this situation goes through excruciating turmoil as they try to weigh their options. They need to hear from a third party that can offer them help and bring clarity to the situation. The couple needs to know that there are people who unconditionally want to love and care for them. These couples need to be shown the "bright side" of the situation as they are provided with all the support they need. Gentleness and kindness need to be demonstrated to these couples who are in such a fragile state. In this way, the couples might be more prone to trust us so that they can more effectively get the help they need. The main focus of the prolife movement is to gently show the life-giving alternatives for the couple. Of course, nothing can be forced, but it can be offered. With the combination of prayer and charity we can hope that the couple will find the courage to choose life for their baby.

Prolife work is a delicate balance that involves supporting and guiding the parents with gentleness and love. As a result, the safety and care of the baby can be met as the parents witness the gift of their "little baby." This is a movement of love and life. People who fight for the right to abort their babies have clouded reason that is distorted by selfishness and a lack of hope. Many times people give reasons to abort that have to do directly with them and not the child whatsoever. Common objections are: I am in college, what about my education? I cannot afford a child right now, or what about my career? There are many other reasons. However, they seem to be blinded by their own desires because their alternative is the death of a child. Is life disposable?

The prolife movement is a movement of love! The heart of the prolife movement says, "Regardless of your circumstance we want to help you and your baby!" We will support you with love and care during this difficult time. We want to remind you of the joys of motherhood and the bliss that your baby will bring you. This movement is all about being there for each other. At no time should any mother ever feel so hopeless that she sees no other alternative but to abort her baby. This is a movement of love that wishes to celebrate the gift of life!

As people walked in the nation's capital holding their signs, singing their songs and praying their prayers, it was evident that our country is prolife, even though the secular media will decide to ignore us, the liberal politicians will turn a deaf ear to us, and the abortion industry will continue to prey on women while they are in an insecure state. We have come together this day to let all of America know that we are prolife and we will never go away! The countless buses that have made the trip across the country, the innumerable sacrifices that people have made only strengthen our movement. This was evident when you witnessed the varied distances that people traveled just to be here. The age range was quite vast as well when you would see infants in their strollers and elderly people in their wheelchairs.

The most obvious sign of hope was the young people as they sang and chanted, lifting their joy-filled voices without hesitation as they carried an optimistic message of courage. This enthusiasm filled the air and reminded all of us that we are celebrating the gift of life. After all, that is what this day is all about, right? We are called to be a witness to "Life!" Committing ourselves to the unborn, to their parents, and to the Lord is necessary. The Lord calls us to defend life as He is the Lord, the Giver of Life.

Next year, when January approaches you might ask yourself, should I go to the March for Life? Without hesitation your answer should be Yes! As a people of life we need to stand up for life in the public square. We need to be a witness to life! We need to do this at the annual March for Life, and all year long in our local homes. How can we do this? We need both prayer and action. First we need prayer, most especially to the Mother of us all, Mother Mary. Under the title, "Our Lady of Guadalupe," our Lady is pregnant with our Lord and she will intercede for us as we seek her motherly guidance. Next, we need to act and that means going forth to these abortion facilities to pray, counsel, and witness to "life," in the public square.

A good friend of mine shared a beautiful experience he had one time at an abortion facility. He felt the Lord urging him to go to pray at an abortion facility one Saturday morning. He was reluctant to go and really wanted to stay in his warm, comfortable bed. However, the Lord kept on "tapping him on the shoulder gently but persistently. Finally, somewhat reluctantly, he decided to crawl out of bed. He drove down to the abortion facility with eyes half-opened as he shook off the "morning cobwebs." Once he arrived, he noticed that nobody was there to pray or counsel the couples. He was the only one there!

He decided to pray his rosary across the street. He knelt down. Some time went by, and he noticed a young couple talking to one another quite intently. He remained praying, and the young couple eventually walked across the street and approached him. They had come over to tell him that they decided to keep their baby, and it was because that he was there. His presence made all the difference! His simple witness to life saved a life and not a single word was uttered. His witness to life was enough.

I love this story because it makes it clear that God is calling all of us to be a witness to life. You do not have to worry about having the right words or anything like that. Simply go forth and pray. Then, let the Lord inspire and direct you. Let the Giver of Life give you direction. In this way, we will all stand together as a "People of Life."

3 THE POWER OF ONE

Was there ever a time when you felt very strongly about a particular conviction and all of a sudden you began to realize that you were surrounded by a large number of people who felt quite differently?

Soon your vigor becomes lukewarm as your lips close before the dreadful possibility that you will be met openly with disdain and scorn. An inward battle takes place between courage and fear.

The voice of courage urges you to speak because "fear" is a coward that tries to discourage us. You find yourself restless with being silent as you pray for strength. Deep inside, you know you must speak out, and you must do so with conviction and compassion.

One day a brave 16-year-old girl found herself in this exact situation quite unexpectedly.

It happened in school. The topic was abortion. The teacher asked for a show of hands when she asked the class collectively, "Who here is pro-choice?"

Twenty of the students raised their hands without hesitation and perhaps without much thought either.

However, there was one hand that did not rise.

When the teacher asked who was anti-abortion, one hand solely raised up against the popular tide. This brave little hand rose up into the air as if to say, "I represent all the tiny hands of the babies in the womb."

And as her hand rose ... so did her voice! She simply stated the truth that we are talking about a baby and that life must be protected and cherished.

At first, her classmates were not convinced, and it was clear that they were ignorant about what takes place in the womb for 9 months. They simply were unaware of the scientific evidence that has shown us that a baby has a heartbeat at 20 days. This fact and many others the 20 students learned about over the course of the next few weeks.

This brave student explained that the little baby in the womb has a right to life just as much as any of us do. In fact, since the baby has no defenses and no voice, we have a moral obligation to defend him or her and to support couples by encouraging them to choose life for their baby.

She also made the point that this topic can be discussed as a human rights issue. She wanted to make it clear because individuals that tend to be pro-choice have a habit of attempting to make this a religious issue, when, in fact, it can be spoken about on a purely scientific level. The journey that we all make through the womb is fascinating, and if people took the time to discover the miracle of life that is growing within during these 9 months, abortion would not even be a consideration.

Did the voice of this brave soul fall on deaf ears?

Thankfully, no, and it was evident by the response of her classmates.

The 20 students who had declared themselves as being pro-choice received a tutorial on life in the womb from their classmate. Now, *14 out of the 20* classmates have had a change of heart and call themselves prolifers.

On that very "regular" school day, a voice did speak and it spoke on behalf of millions of voiceless babies. That brave, young woman is named Bari.

What would have happened if Bari chose to be silent? What would have happened if Bari got intimidated by her classmates? *What would have happened if Bari decided to take the easy way out?*

If Bari remained silent, 20 of her peers and her teacher would never have learned about the beauty of life in the womb. Now 14 other individuals can be a voice for the voiceless thanks to Bari.

Personally, I have been inspired by Bari, and when her grandmother, Anne, told me this story I was highly enthused and knew immediately that I needed to write about it.

Bari is a brave soul and we live in times that are in great need for such souls. By her example, she has showed us that by conviction and compassion even the most hardened hearts can melt and embrace the truth about life. People hunger for the truth even when they appear disinterested.

As a people of life, we need to speak up! We need to pray for the courage to speak and the grace to do it with love. We never need to feel insecure or unsure about ourselves. This is God's work and He will supply the words for us. We only need to calmly and patiently be witnesses to the truth -- about Life!

The heart of our message is that life is a gift, a celebration ... a great cause for joy! As we defend life let us do it with great joy and peace.

One day, a high-school teacher asked a question that would radically change the way her students would think forever. Yet the students were not so much changed by the question, but instead by *the answer of one.*

Special thanks to Bari!

4 A MOTHER'S HEART
A TRIBUTE TO ALL MOTHERS

From the very beginning of motherhood, a mother begins to sacrifice. Her entire life becomes a life of sacrificial love.

Just about the time a woman realizes that she is pregnant, she may begin to experience morning sickness. Throughout her pregnancy she gives up her vanity as her "little one" increases in size. Physical discomfort becomes the norm as sitting and walking become more challenging as time goes on. Then, the pains of giving birth demand the attention of the mother entirely as her muscles contract and her will is tested beyond bravery.

Now, this new person is in the arms of his mother, and her "bundle of joy" fills her heart with much gratitude. From this day onward, there is no rest for the "new" mom. Her new schedule will be anything but regular, and spontaneous interruptions will be the new norm. There will be no such thing as a daily time schedule that is consistent and reliable. Her baby is here and is completely dependent upon her.

The baby's needs overshadow all of the mom's needs, and mom begins a string of sacrifices that will quickly become second nature for her. This new "little creature" will wake up at will, cry when he is hungry, and naturally will cry when something is amiss. Morning or evening is irrelevant to this little guy, and more than likely his demands will be made at inopportune times.

Only the love of a mother can be so attentive to these demanding needs. A love that is patient, persistent, and perpetual. Her primary concern is her little baby, and mom lovingly takes second place from now on. She does this willingly and without any hesitation.

As time goes on and the days swiftly turn into years, the cares of the mother continue to change. The terrible two's, accompanied with teething and the growth of new language skills, bring about a new set of concerns, as the baby becomes a toddler who is increasingly more active.

When the child becomes five and ready for school he will be confronted with new challenges. These will be primarily concerns regarding socialization skills as he is now surrounded by peers who will also be adapting to their new environment. These many "little personalities" will learn how to interact with one another as they attempt to communicate their needs and wants in an affable manner. Another significant issue at this time can be separation anxiety from both their mother and home. A new environment, new people, and a new schedule are quite a bit to suddenly become acclimated to all at once for any little guy. All the while mom is at home worrying about her little one, as she knows she needs to start letting go so that he can grow.

The years of primary school continue as the days are filled with soccer games, piano lessons, and homework. The early teenage years bring about social awkwardness as teens begin to become increasingly preoccupied with the opposite sex. Their bodies continue to change and grow, sometimes at an alarming rate. Now mom, who was "clinged to" for over a decade, has now become a figure to avoid.

As the teenage years continue, this little guy has now become an adolescent who is starving for more and more independence. Little does he know that with freedom comes increased responsibility. These teenage years will bring with them "new" socialization challenges. Being "cool" and accepted among his peers will be the new goal for a teenager. During these years, mom has to be a counselor, psychologist, and life coach. She has to let go of her own ingrained desires to protect her boy and let him learn from his own experiences.

As high school graduation quickly approaches, the teenager has to rapidly grow up as he is presented with new decisions that will forever affect his future. These decisions no longer involve subjects like who he should go to the prom with. No, now these decisions will involve the beginning of his adulthood.

The nature of these decisions carries more weight as this young adult has his future slowly unfold in front of him. Here, mom continues to let go as she keeps a watchful eye on her "little one." Perhaps the "letting go," is the most difficult part for mom but she also knows innately that it is the best for her son so that he can grow into the man he will become. The days of foolishly running around with his friends are coming to a close as the realization of a career or long-term goal becomes paramount. During these years the love of a mother is at times painfully silent as she sees her son who was once her "little boy" growing up before her. She shows us all that perhaps the greatest sacrifice of all is the "letting go."

As this young man enters into the beginning of a new career which marks his introduction into the workforce, his mom proudly looks on from the distance. Her love compels her to be more distant from her son so that he can grow more in this new stage of life.

As the years continue, a mother soon will be met with perhaps her most difficult challenge. One day her son will bring home a young lady who will become his future wife. A mother will be met with ambivalent feelings as her joy is mingled with sorrow. The sacrifice will involve letting go once again, which never really gets easy. However, overriding those feelings will be the joy of her son's newfound love which will lead to a son or daughter of his own.

Now, the joy of a mother has entered into a new level of joy, which is the joy of a grandmother.

As we briefly touched upon the many stages of motherhood, we saw how all throughout it a mother loves sacrificially. Throughout her motherhood the challenges change but she meets each challenge with unconditional love. She knows when to push and when to let go. She desires to see her child grow, and she knows that in order for that to happen she must sacrifice. That sacrifice will also hurt but, as a result, it will bring forth growth in her child.

To me the love of a mother is incomparable. It is a love that does not think of itself. It is a love that gives until it hurts. It is a love that we can all depend on. For these reasons, a mother's heart is truly one that is set apart.

5 ONE LOOK
IN HONOR OF OUR FATHERS

As we approach Father's Day, there is a story that depicts the fortitude that many of our fathers unknowingly possess. It is a story of strength, determination, and commitment.

One evening, a woman who just turned 30 decided to go out and celebrate her three decades of life. On this night, she went to a bar and met a man whom she would eventually have intimate relations with. She learned soon thereafter that she was pregnant.

She was a bit anxious naturally. However, she was also strong, and she knew that she wanted her baby.

However, when she told the father, he vehemently denied the baby was his. He wanted nothing to do with it. Nevertheless, the mother was determined to keep her baby, and she made it clear that she would do anything for her child, with or without the help of the father.

This mother had a very good career, which she knew she would have to leave for the time being for her baby. This was not an issue for her regardless of her many career accomplishments.

She stood her ground as the father continued to deny that the baby was his. As she insisted that it was truly his baby without a doubt, he became more entrenched in his stance with no intention to budge.

The mother's love only grew stronger as her baby was growing within her. She exemplified the strength and beauty of motherhood. This mother shows us all that love does not see the problems, but only the solutions to the problems. "Love bears all things."

Meanwhile, the father continued to be distant as his heart grew colder.

Finally, the day of birth arrived and, with it, the joy of seeing the newborn baby. A mother and child were united in love!

It was sad that the father of the baby was not there. But the prayers of the mother must have reached the ears of some attentive angels that day.

Later that day, the father of the baby came to the hospital to see his newborn child. It took *one look*, and the father was instantly drawn to his son. From that moment, the father found his reason for living. Later, the mother would say that the boy's father was absolutely enthralled with his son.

Five years have passed since and this little baby united his father and mother. Ever since that first moment in the hospital, the boy's father has been a dedicated and devout father.

What was it that changed the father's heart? Was it the look of innocence? Was it the look of vulnerability? Was it the look of purity?

One thing we know for sure was that it only took one look!

On this Father's Day, let us honor all of those fathers out there who have tirelessly loved us without reservation.

The love of a father is shown quite differently as compared with the love of a mother. At first, this father was filled with fear, apprehension, and denial. But once he saw the beauty of his child before his own eyes, he realized that his life was forever changed. It was no longer about him, but it was all about his child.

This is the type of love we want to acknowledge on this Father's Day. It is this love that works overtime so that his child can have a better life. It is this love that protects his child as he teaches him how to be independent. Most of all, it is this love that affirms the child, showing him that he truly believes in him.

Thank you to all the fathers who are the silent anchors that keep our homes from drifting into turbulent weather.

6 IS AMERICA PROLIFE?

Is America prolife? If you want to find out, go out into the streets and the people will tell you.

As they do this, they display prolife signs to remind people of the injustice that is committed daily in this country.

When I have been praying with my fellow prolife friends, I've noticed that the majority of the feedback we receive from the public is overwhelmingly positive. Only rarely will somebody feel the need to be rude with a vulgar comment. When movements are grown from the "grassroots," you really get a good sense of how the people in the nation really feel.

I believe most Americans believe in the rights of the unborn. Approximately, 4,000 babies are aborted every day as the rest of us enjoy our days in peace and freedom. If America is the land of the free, why are the unborn denied this privilege?

Deep down Americans know that abortion is wrong.

Of course, the mass media chooses to ignore this as they provide quite a "slanted liberal view," with the hopes of deceiving the people.

The truth cannot be ignored, though. Even when couples go for an abortion, they frequently express sorrow for what they are about to do and then proceed with ambivalence. If it wasn't morally wrong, they wouldn't have any struggle or trepidation before making such a critical decision. Unfortunately, many couples buy the lie that the abortion industry sells them: *there is no hope.*

That's the same message that the mass media projects.

Of course, this is largely done by layers of lies that distort the truth and even ignore the scientific facts regarding life in the womb. If the mass media were honest, why wouldn't they be open to a debate regarding the matter?

At all costs, they avoid the facts as they deceptively prey on the feelings of those in a precarious situation. They rely on slogans which incite fear in the hearts of those who are in a fragile state. And they manage to manipulate the masses without an honest display of the facts. They falsely give you the impression that most Americans are pro-choice.

Where does this leave us? How do we get out our message of love for both "the woman and the baby?"

I still believe most Americans are prolife and the people who are unsure about the abortion issue only need to be properly educated.

If a person is sincere and willing to look into it with an honest heart, I feel confident they will eventually become prolife.

Personally, I can relate to this because at the age of 20, when I was in college, I had mixed feelings about the subject of abortion.

Deep down I was prolife, but I had a sociology teacher who made statements that confused me.

I respected her and liked her as a teacher. Besides, she was a professional, so I felt that she must be right since she was in a position of authority at a Catholic college. However, my intuition, which has always steered me clear of danger, alerted me with an uneasy feeling about her position which I just could not ignore.

One particular day, she stated, "I think abortion is a horrible thing, really, but I still think that people have the right to do it if they choose to do so." This just made no sense to me, and it was such a conflicting statement. After all, if abortion is so horrible, then why should anybody have the right to do it? Did she really believe that it was horrible?

Since she was my professor I respected her, but I still had doubt within me. I struggled with this and it kept gnawing at me. I knew that I needed to get to the bottom of this, and I could not continue feeling ambivalent on this issue. It was just too important!

One day it happened! It actually seemed to happen by accident.

I was watching EWTN (Eternal Word Television Network) as Fr. Frank Pavone, founder of Priests for Life, was speaking on abortion. Around this time, the late Cardinal John O'Connor, of the Archdiocese of New York, gave Fr. Pavone the specific apostolate of educating others on abortion.

Ironically, it seemed that Catholics needed this education just as much as anybody else. The episode I saw was so enlightening. It was as if Fr. Pavone lifted the veil of lies and exposed the truth about abortion in an instant.

One thing that he said, which I've always remembered, was that the pro-choice stance never ever wants to speak about the act of abortion. They are willing to talk to you about a variety of circumstances, such as extreme situations, but they will never talk about the actual act of abortion. As they avoid this particular aspect of the topic, they will talk to you about everything else as they engineer the language to best suit their needs.

As an example, it is much more comfortable to say the "termination of a pregnancy," as compared with what it truly is: the "killing of a baby." Sugarcoating the reality does not change that reality, nor does it lessen the guilt associated with the act. Denial does not help anyone as it continues the injustice and prevents the need for necessary healing.

After listening to Fr. Pavone, I felt so relieved, and I could now see everything so clearly. Consequently, this knowledge demanded that I do something, and it was the birth of my own involvement in the prolife movement.

Another important point that Fr. Pavone has made for many years is that people need to see abortion in order to have their hearts changed. Many times he has said, "Once Americans see the horror of abortion . . . they will become prolife."

I really believe that this is most especially true. Pictures say more than words can at times. This is certainly true when an injustice is taking place. Of course, nobody wants to see an aborted baby. However, sometimes we need to see something that is so horrific that it inspires us to move out of our mold of complacency.

Most Americans are too complacent about abortion as we have let it settle into our cultural landscape. The time of urgency is now. We need to get off of our couches and into the streets. The time to pray and counsel those who are most in need is now!

Is America prolife?

Without hesitation I would say so. We need to educate the American people and pray so that their hearts may be open to receive the truth about "Life." Then together as a country we can be truly united as we fight for freedom for all of our citizens, including the unborn. The ugliness of abortion will be banished from this land as the beauty of a newborn child rightfully replaces it.

As Americans, we can then proudly stand next to one another as we declare liberty and justice for all.

7 WHAT ARE YOU TALKING ABOUT?

A few weeks ago, I heard a disturbing story on the news. Equally disturbing was the cavalier manner in which it was reported on the radio.

It was about a woman who went into labor at a nightclub. She gave birth in the bathroom and then suffocated the baby and hid the body in the toilet tank. Afterwards, she smoked a cigarette and then returned to the bar as if nothing happened. The next morning, the baby was found by a maintenance worker.

The indifference expressed by the reporter telling the story left an unsettled feeling in my stomach. There was a callousness to her voice, which was void of compassion – and even normal emotion.

Her tone seemed to imply that if a mother finds a baby to be an inconvenience, she can simply just get rid of him. It made me wonder if the reporter understood the gravity of the situation.

Is this what 40 years of abortion on demand have done to us? Has our country lost its sensitivity to the sacredness of life?

Perhaps. If our land allows a mother to kill her own child, then why wouldn't life become so cheap?

It's obvious that over the years the number of stories of violent acts against the innocent and defenseless has grown. The elderly are victims of euthanasia. The disabled are neglected and even abused. Unwanted babies are left unattended to cry themselves to their final breath.

Now it seems that when these horribly sad stories hit the airwaves, many people – like the reporter — are just desensitized to such tragedies.

What has numbed so many Americans to the atrocities that lie before us? Have we gotten so accustomed to the killings that we accept them as part of the American landscape? Do we excuse ourselves by simply saying, "That does not involve me"?

There are many answers to these questions but I think, in large part, the media has been responsible for this desensitization.

They've done it by shifting our attention on matters. The important or even grave issues they downplay as if they are trivial. Then, they place an ever-increasing importance on silly matters that are largely from the entertainment industry.

Just put on the television or the radio and you'll see this demonstrated as people talk passionately about some sports or entertainment star.

Turn the A.M. dial on the radio and you'll hear people discussing their favorite player or team with so much fervor that they might even start yelling or hang up the phone out of anger!

On television it's the Hollywood celebrities! We adorn them with applause and awards and look to them as role models as we follow their every move as documented in magazines and entertainment shows.

Our attention becomes consumed by a fantasy world, based on the lives of people who act or play sports for a living. And this escape is at the expense of the real matters, which aren't always easy to look at but, nevertheless, demand our attention.

It was my 10-year-old niece who brought this home to me. One day she was watching how baseball fans on television reacted to a home run.

In her eyes, she saw their response as an overreaction. With a pure innocence and wisdom she stated, "Big deal, he hit a ball with a bat … how silly, everybody gets so excited over that?"

When she said this she unknowingly made me re-think my own passions. As I looked in the mirror I had to ask myself, "Am I as passionate in life about important issues as I am about this team?" Were my values in the right order? Her comment caused me to take inventory of what was important to me.

And I think this is something we all must do as we confront a society where the lives of those in Hollywood grow in importance, while the lives of the vulnerable and innocent are increasingly discounted.

We must put what is important in the forefront again!

We must remind people of the atrocity of 4,000 abortions which occur in our own country each day. We must offer help and support to a pregnant mother.

This will help bring the sanctity of life back to the forefront of our discussions both in our own house and the White House. Let's get busy talking about what matters so that our words can lead us to action. And, in this way, our actions will lead us to the saving of innocent human lives.

8 THE WINGS TO FLY

When the Catholic Church had an abundance of vocations it sent out missionaries throughout the world.

But the Church knew that prayer must come before action. So in her wisdom she arranged for religious orders that had a special charism for prayer — holy monks and nuns in the monasteries and cloisters — to pray earnestly for the missions.

In this way, the souls of the people the missionaries would come in contact with would be well prepared to receive the graces God offers. This is similar to what happens in our own lives when we seek out God's guidance through prayer, which will lead us to the action we need to take next.

This idea is very important for the prolife movement as well. In the public square, we need both prayer and action. By action, I specifically mean counseling. It might be tempting to think that we only need one or the other. Usually, this is not the case.

Prayer, most especially to Our Lady through the Holy Rosary, is so powerful. After all, she is the Mother of us all. Shouldn't we implore the Mother of Humanity to help all mothers in distress, as well as their little babies?

The need for prayer at abortion sites cannot be stressed enough. As we pray for the hearts of those contemplating abortion, we ask that their hearts may soften so that they can see the hope that belongs to them.

But action is imperative too! We need to have counselors guiding and consoling couples considering an abortion.

Some people feel directly called to do this work. Others may first go to an abortion site only to pray, but as time goes on, they may feel more open to the idea of counseling. Sometimes people just need to get familiar with the setting, and when they do, they may get more involved by talking to women in need.

Counseling does not always leave you with "warm and fuzzy" feelings. Honestly, it involves rejection, hostile temperaments, and sometimes an open resentment for your presence there.

However, there are times when a woman decides to turn around and choose life for her baby. Sometimes you might have an in-depth conversation with a person that leads them closer to the Lord. When these things happen, it is clear that God is at work.

In my opinion, the most important aspect of counseling is answering the call to be a "sign of hope" for these couples. They may not accept your invitation to help them, but the important thing is that the invitation was given.

To me the saddest thing is when a couple feels trapped because they were never offered help. This should never happen! This is why answering the call to counsel is crucial and not to be taken lightly.

There is much to say about counseling, but the most important thing to remember is to continuously seek the Holy Spirit.

The Holy Spirit will let you know what to say, when to say it, and how to say it.

There have been numerous times that I went to say something to someone but nothing came out of my mouth. The Lord knows the heart of His creatures. Perhaps, that person was not meant to be spoken to at that particular time. In our society, we place so much value on the spoken word. However, sometimes silence has a value . . . a deeper value that goes beyond our understanding.

Counseling must include the following: compassion, gentleness, a sense of urgency, and a willingness to help at all costs.

For an eagle to soar above the land in the high skies it needs to have two wings. Then, it can survey the land and see more clearly what lies beneath it. This is also true for those involved in the prolife movement. We too need the two essential wings of prayer and counseling so that we can effectively touch the hearts of those we come in contact with. We need prayer to soften the heart and counseling to guide it.

As this takes place, we will soar to new heights as hearts open to the gift of new life. Let our message of hope and love fly throughout the world so that life may be cherished everywhere.

9 THE SOLUTION TO RESOLUTIONS

Many times when we're really motivated to get something done we tend to overlook the very tools we need to accomplish our goal. And one of the most fundamental and obvious things that somehow gets lost in our enthusiasm is to remember to include God in our endeavors.

I've made this mistake countless times — going forward with my own agenda without ever seeking direction from God. I felt that I had it all together, and perhaps I would talk to God about it at a later date ... and that's just what I end up doing, usually after things are falling apart in my hands.

But in hindsight, it was clear that the heartache or difficulty I went through was caused by my own stubbornness. Eating humble pie is no fun, but the lesson surely leaves its mark on your soul. So I've resolved that from now on, instead of running off aimlessly with my own ideas, I'm going to include God before the adventure starts, so that it won't turn out to be a disaster.

But how can I effectively do this on a daily basis? How can I make it work?

Commitment to a daily Holy Hour! That's the answer for me.

For example, take my good friend, Ken. For years now he has spent countless hours in adoration of the Blessed Sacrament. At some point, he made a conscious decision to give the Lord a "Holy Hour" every single day.

In order to do this consistently, he picked a time of the day that worked best for him. And now, when 10 p.m. approaches, everything else stops for Ken. He enters the doors of the chapel, and from 10 to 11 p.m. every night he spends that time being with the Lord in silent adoration.

He made this commitment 10 years ago. This resolution took time to master, and it involved some sacrifices. But now it is second nature for him, and that hour belongs solely to the Lord.

Now, as we all know from our experience with New Year's resolutions, there's always the temptation to get discouraged too quickly and give up.

Even as I acknowledge the spiritual reality that strength comes from the Lord and that I will find it there in adoration of Him, I still have to deal with my lazy nature, which would often rather just relax with a cup of coffee or get some more sleep.

I know that, on my part, I need to take responsibility and commit to a realistic hour daily. If friends are expecting me for dinner, wouldn't I make an effort to be there? Being a "no-show" would let them down. The same should be true for Christ in adoration. He is our true friend and we want to treat Him as such.

Perhaps going to adoration with a cause in mind can give us even more motivation because it places responsibility on us. So why not go to adoration for the unborn? Why not pray for their protection? For their confused parents? Why not pray for the people who work in the abortion facility so that they may have a change of heart?

These unborn babies depend on me, and I have an obligation to be there for them. Similarly, I now have an obligation to console Our Lord for the sin of abortion. By increasing my time in adoration, I am able to decrease the senseless acts of abortion.

This idea of making a daily Holy Hour as a New Year's resolution is very exciting to me for many reasons. It is a concrete act that simply requires me to get myself to the chapel at an hour of my own choosing. Once I am there the Lord will guide me, and I just need to allow myself to be "open" so that I can truly listen.

The benefits of adoration are endless. Through this devotion I hope to become a "chiseled instrument" for the Lord so that His Will may be done in my life.

By going to adoration I receive guidance, healing, and insight as the Lord reveals Himself to me. When we look at the unborn and Jesus in the Blessed Sacrament we see many similarities. They are both innocent, pure, defenseless, silent, and holy.

I believe all of these factors will be inspiring to us as we decide to commit to a daily "Holy Hour."

Do it for yourself, for the unborn, for those who are despairing, for the sick, for the dying and, most of all, for the Lord. In the Garden of Gethsemane, Jesus was left alone to pray in His agony when His disciples fell asleep. As he once asked them, He is asking us now, "Could you not keep watch for One Hour with me?"

What will your answer be?

10 GOOD MORNING

Once on a beautiful Saturday morning, I overheard a woman say good morning to a co-worker.

This is something we all hear every day as we exchange pleasantries with loved ones and even total strangers.

However, on this particular day the echo of those words stayed with me.

These were people who worked at an abortion facility. I was close by, attempting to give out prolife literature so that couples would choose life for their baby.

Hearing that cheerful exclamation of "good morning" left me in a melancholy mood. Never would these innocent unborn babies hear a "good morning" from anybody ... ever! The irony of it all was striking. Here it was a beautiful morning, warm greetings were being exchanged — and the cold reality for the unborn nearby was unthinkable.

In the matter of an hour or so these defenseless victims would be brutally dismantled in their mother's wombs. There would be no morning for these babies, as there could be nothing good that could come from this act of brutality. Who would mourn for these forgotten victims? Would anybody remember them today or tomorrow?

Now, whenever I say or hear "good morning," I can't help but think of these little ones who have been robbed of their bright mornings here on earth.

So now, when the morning sun rises and God sheds His light upon us all I try to be mindful that He has blessed me with a "good morning," and my heart should be filled with gratitude. The Lord, "the Giver of Life," has granted us a "good morning," and I wish to make it good for Him.

One of the ways to do this is to remember the unborn in our thoughts and prayers.

Another is to pray that couples in need will find the strength and courage to choose life. If it's possible, I will witness to life where it is needed most, in the public square. This is where we will find the distraught couple. This is where we can help the helpless baby. This is where we can offer our support and truly wish to those in need a sincere "good morning."

11 LIMITLESS LOVE

The winter of 2014 will be remembered as a time of endless snowstorms and freezing cold temperatures. The Northeast was relentlessly battered with frigid weather that made even a short walk to the car feel like an eternity.

It made me wonder how the homeless handle such harsh weather all winter long.

It's so easy to forget about them once we get inside our heated homes. But I recently overheard a remarkable conversation that showed me that one person had not forgotten about their plight.

My good friend Colleen (I'm not using real names) mentioned that she recently found out that a man she knows was homeless. To my amazement, in her next breath, she said that she had some empty bedrooms in her home, and she was going to offer him shelter as he seeks employment.

She said this without any hesitation, as she willingly and lovingly shared her joy in offering help to this homeless man. Her solution to the problem was simple – and immediate. And this is the heart of the prolife message. Love requires sacrifice, and true love does not count the cost.

Colleen was like Mary, a young woman who has made a tremendous impact in the prolife movement.

From the very beginning, her deep commitment and enthusiasm bore fruit as she counseled couples that were seeking an abortion. Her sincerity and passion touched the hearts of many young women, who decided to keep their babies.

But she didn't stop there. Mary stayed by their side throughout their pregnancies. She prayed with them, counseled them, and comforted them in difficult times. There were many trips to the doctor's office, and she would translate for them when there was a language barrier.

Her love required a great deal of sacrifice, and her commitment shows us all how to love without reservation.

Another good friend, Bridget, was instrumental in convincing a young woman to keep her baby.

Bridget spent an entire day helping this young woman find a place to live and get the support that she needed. However, for Bridget this was only the beginning. She kept in close touch with her young friend for the next 6 months.

She got a stroller, diapers, a playpen, and pretty much anything a new baby needs. It seemed as if she never slept because she was always on the move … ready to help.

The day the baby was born Bridget was at the hospital, making a list of more items she planned to get for this joyous mother. In fact, the young mother told me," Bridget has been there for me every step of the way. If I need something, she is always there."

Bridget and her inexhaustible energy exemplified her love. This was a love that knew no bounds.

Colleen, Mary, and Bridget solve the problems they find before them by simply loving. All of their stories are great witnesses to the prolife movement.

The characteristic that personally struck me the most in all three was not the tireless work they did. It was how they answered "the call" to love without any hesitation or reservation.

There were no questions asked. Instead, they acted immediately, and the action they all took was to love … to love with a limitless love.

12 THE GIVER OF LIFE

As Christians, we say the Creed every Sunday, and midway through the prayer we acknowledge the Holy Spirit as "the Lord, the Giver of Life."

When we recite familiar prayers, it's easy to say them by rote without thinking. But the "Giver of Life"! These words can stop us in our tracks, when we realize what they really mean.

God is so generous that He allows us to partake in the process of creation. We become co-creators with the Lord, sharing in the dignity of creating our very own children.

As a couple unites, they share an expression of their love that may bring forth fruit, a beautiful baby. And this process of creation — with the power of God — brings forth the creation of a soul, which is more precious to Him than all the stars of the universe. What an honor and what a deep responsibility!

This reality is often lost on modern man. And that perhaps is why he has also lost his reverence for life.

Life has become disposable. If somebody is inconvenient or looked on as a burden, then we take the liberty of simply discarding them. Is life so cheap? Can we just get rid of somebody because we don't want to be bothered with their needs?

If so, what has become of us? For a country with some of the finest educational institutions in the world, it seems as if we've lost our minds collectively as a society. Have we become so smart that we're stupid?

Well, maybe stupid is too harsh, but selfish seems to fit. We are the "me" generation, and we want what we want when we want it. And I think that mentality is what has led us so far from the human touch, the times when people seemed to genuinely care for one another.

What happened? Why is there such a deep hatred running through society? Perhaps we need to implore the Holy Spirit more fervently to replace the fire of hatred with the fire of His love — the true fire that will transform the entire world.

The Lord not only wants to give us life, but to give it to us abundantly. This requires trust, which can be scary at times.

But the Holy Spirit reminds us that the Lord will not give us more than we can handle, that he will strengthen us to do whatever He inspires us to do. We only need to call upon Him so that our despair can be turned to hope and our eyes will be opened to see the beauty of the gift of life.

For the Lord is the giver of all good things. Let us remind every woman who finds herself pregnant and discouraged that the Lord, the Giver of Life, will embrace her with His love and His promise to hold her and her precious little baby in the palm of His hand for all eternity.

13 ONE QUIET MORNING

One quiet morning, a man walking along the street noticed smoke rising above some buildings a few blocks away. He headed toward it merely out of curiosity. But as the smoke became thicker and darker, he picked up his pace.

At the corner, he could see flames coming from a house. Was there no one else around? Had no one reported this? As the seconds ticked by, he realized that he might be the only hope for anyone who might be trapped inside.

As he approached the blaze, a piercing cry from a woman shook him to the core. It was a cry of desperation. *"Please help me and my baby ... please!"*

The man quickly moved into action. There was no time to spare! He charged into the house whose upper stories were already engulfed with flames and, following the cries of the baby and the coughing of the mother, made his way through the smoky hallway.

He found them on the first floor, picked up the mother clinging to her infant, and with determination and unrelenting courage carried them to safety.

Then he helped them to the ambulance, which had just arrived at the scene, and accompanied them to the hospital where they got the medical attention they needed.

The mother was deeply grateful and thanked the gentleman for saving her life and the life of her baby. The man knew that the Lord inspired him from the beginning, as it all happened so quickly.

The above story is not true. However, it's a parable — meant to illustrate an important point.

A woman considering an abortion is like the mother in this story, trapped in a burning building. Usually, she feels very alone. A smoke of confusion clouds her ability to see love. All she can do is cry as the flames surround her and her baby.

She desperately needs help! The smoke that billows out of the building is a sign to all of us that there are women in great need. Although they may be only quietly crying, inside they are screaming for help.

They don't know where to turn for support. We need to be proactive and help them. And that may require all our courage, strength, and selflessness, the same qualities needed to run into a burning building.

Sometimes the call to save a life requires us to get out of our comfort zone. And if we're able to do that, we can greet the unknown — whatever we might encounter on "one quiet morning" — with hope and love.

14 FORGIVENESS

*"Abortion compounds the grief of many women
who now carry with them deep physical and
spiritual wounds after succumbing to the
pressures of a secular culture which devalues
God's gift of sexuality and the right to life of
the unborn."*

-- Pope Francis, April 25, 2014, at a meeting with African bishops.

The grief and pain of abortion's aftermath have devastated the lives of many men and women, who feel they have nowhere to turn.

How horrible it must feel to be forgotten!

How many women are hurting from abortion and feel they have nobody to talk to about their hurt? How many men struggle with their lost fatherhood as they try to handle their own hurt alone? And even couples, trying to navigate their way through a sea of stormy emotions, may find themselves feeling isolated.

Does the abortion industry concern itself with them at all? The answer is simply No! Once they receive their money and perform the abortion they point to the door.

And what happens when a woman leaves after her abortion is truly heart breaking to witness. More than once I've seen women come out of an abortion facility devastated. Some wail. Others take a few steps, only to collapse in despair on the sidewalk.

What I've seen will be forever in my mind, stirring a mixture of emotions. The strongest is sorrow for these women. But there's also a horrible feeling of helplessness inside — and anger grows. This anger asks, "How can the abortionists and other people responsible for this justify themselves?"

These women, who have been so exploited and then abandoned in their fragile emotional state, need to know that there is help!

This is where we in the prolife movement can come in. We need to show couples that the time for forgiveness is now. And if they feel they're not worthy to be forgiven, we need to remind them that Christ died for *all* our sins – not just for some of them.

We need to assure them that the Lord loves and forgives and that their healing is of utmost importance to Him.

Perhaps we can direct them to Rachel's Vineyard, a group that offers weekend retreats that focus on forgiveness and healing for both men and women. They have helped countless people to mend their lives.

And that hope of mending brings to my mind the saying "For those that love God, everything will be used for their betterment."

Perhaps, somewhere down the road, it may be possible that those who've experienced abortion first hand can use their pain to help others.

In no way am I suggesting that this would not be difficult to do. But if a woman who has had an abortion could find the strength to counsel other women who are considering an abortion, it would be most powerful.

She could share her experience, her words would have a tremendous impact, and through her a life could be saved.

Therefore, let us pray that those who are grieving a child lost to abortion will run to the healing "Heart of Jesus" so His forgiveness will allow them to go forward. And perhaps they will even become His instruments as they steer other women on the path of truth to embrace the gift of life!

15 A CULTURE OF LIFE

It's hard to believe that 15 years ago the tragedy at Columbine took place. On April 20, 1999, two teenagers went into their school intending to cause absolute chaos by killing innocent students and staff. Twelve students and one teacher lost their lives.

America has changed drastically since that event. Violence seems to have increased in frequency and intensity. Now, it's not uncommon to see school shootings. We've seen horrific attacks in movie theaters, malls, and even on busy street corners. Violence is the new norm on the American landscape. Recently, a young teenage boy took the life of a classmate because she did not say "yes" to his prom invitation.

How can we trust each other when the climate of today's society is so filled with rage and unpredictability?

In order to restore trust and hope, a renewed reverence for the sanctity of life must find a place again in our minds and hearts – a "Culture of Life."

The world has been blessed with two prolife leaders who by their words and actions showed us all the importance of reverencing life: Mother Teresa and St. John Paul II.

What did they have to say about the sanctity of life?

Mother Teresa had a way of stating a profound truth with such simplicity. For example, she once said, "How can there be too many children? That is like saying there are too many flowers."

But, at times, her simplicity could be direct and dire:

"If we accept that a mother can kill even her own child, how can we tell other people to not kill each other? Any country that accepts abortion is not teaching its people to love, but to use any violence to get what they want."

Mother Teresa did not shy away from telling pro-choice politicians these truths. She firmly and gently spoke the truth regardless of how it was received. The Lord gave her a courageous spirit that did not seek the honor of men but, instead, a faithfulness to the truth.

Pope John Paul II also wrote and spoke in defense of the sacredness of human life in all its stages, from conception to natural death. Like Mother Teresa, he was not afraid to address the entire world: "A nation that kills its own children is a nation without a future."

His actions were as grace-filled as his words.

In the last stages of his life Pope John Paul II suffered with Parkinson's disease. It was quite noticeable, and his speech was so affected it was nearly impossible for him to speak intelligibly to the great masses that assembled to see him in St. Peter's Square.

It would have been much easier for him to politely decline to appear in public. However, he did not do this. Instead, he gave another message on "life." In his frailty, he showed the world his vulnerability by appearing to the crowds even though he was unable to communicate as he once could.

His actions spoke loud and clear: Human life is holy and sacred even when, or especially when, we are most vulnerable.

Mother Teresa too showed that all human life is precious regardless of the circumstances. Mother had a special love for the dying. She saw to it that the dying would receive the utmost dignity and respect up until their final moment.

One story illustrates this beautifully. One day a man who lived in the slums was dying in the gutter, covered with maggots. Mother Teresa took him in and cleaned him up. The nuns treated him with great care! Before he died he said to Mother, "Before I lived like an animal on the streets, but today I will die like an angel." The care that Mother Teresa gave him restored to him his human dignity.

The struggle between a "Culture of Life" and a "Culture of Death" continues in our society. At times, we can be tempted to despair when we witness the tragedies that play out before our eyes.

However, God gave us two spiritual leaders for our time who are now interceding on our behalf in Heaven. Mother Teresa and John Paul II showed us that the remedy to "The Culture of Death" is not destruction but love — unconditional love that requires sacrifice but does not count the cost.

We need to heed the words of Pope Saint John Paul II: "Be not afraid!"

With these three powerful words he challenged each and every one of us to declare "The Gospel of Life" without reservation.

In order to overcome this "Culture of Death," we need to bring hope where there is despair, light where there is darkness, and love where there is hatred. By doing this we will restore the "Culture of Life" in our society, one heart at a time.

16 SIDEWALK COUNSELING

Sidewalk counseling outside an abortion clinic – human lives are at stake, and you're on the front lines. You may be the last lifeline of hope for a pregnant woman as she approaches the building to abort her child. She and those with her tend to be in a fragile state, wrestling with conflicting emotions. Things can happen quickly.

Knowing what to say and how to say it is of utmost importance. It can make the difference between a person accepting your help or walking away.

If you're considering becoming a part of this important work, I'd like to share with you a few of the important things I've learned. I've been counseling for 20 years now. And just like anything else, the more experience one has -- well, it never gets easy but it does get less difficult.

The Approach

How should you approach a couple who are seeking an abortion?

First, It's important to understand where they're coming from. Their emotions are in turmoil, overwhelming and volatile.

Internally, they've been going through a battle between what they're tempted to do and what they should do. And now that they've decided to come to the abortion facility, many of them feel the question of whether or not to go through with the abortion has been resolved.

At this point, they just want to get this experience over with quickly so that they can get on with their lives and forget about the entire ordeal.

But, to their surprise, they see individuals on the sidewalk who appear to be standing in their way. A bunch of "religious zealots," they think, who

42

only want to harass them and make them feel guilty and add to the heavy burden that rests on their shoulders.

So how should we, the sidewalk counselors, respond?

Since the couple already feels defensive, it's important to dispel their illusions about us. We need to get across that we're there for one reason only: to help them.

It's been said that within the first few seconds of meeting you, a stranger makes a good number of judgments about you. Body language is a language unto itself, and it reveals a great deal. So smile. A smile has the power to knock down barriers that are otherwise immoveable. In a smile we see that a person is glad to see us. By welcoming the couple with a smile you are inviting them to dialogue with you.

Then approach them gently but with a sense of urgency in your voice reflecting the seriousness of the situation. It's also helpful to slightly bend down to them so as to present a manner that won't be perceived as threatening.

I tell them that we can help them, and it won't cost them a cent. If there's a pregnancy center nearby (and there often are near abortion mills), let them know where it is and strongly recommend that they consider seeking help there in making such a grave decision. Make it clear that these services are free.

If they don't want to engage with you, gently encourage them to take the literature you have for them so that they can look through it as they wait in the abortion facility. In this way, they may be touched by what they read since they are not open to a discussion at the moment. The idea is that they get the prolife message one way or another.

Making an Informed Decision

If the couple is willing to talk with you, an important point to bring up early on is that they need to make an informed decision.

As an analogy, when people decide to buy a car, they don't buy it simply because it looks good. Instead, they find out about the miles per gallon, the safety features, the size, and all the other important details. Then, with all of the facts before them, they can make a truly informed decision.

Well, if this is true about a mere car, which is only a "thing," how much more important is it when a human life is at stake?

To make an informed decision, people need to know the facts about the baby in the womb. You may need to present this information and make them aware of the scientific reality of life in the womb.

Pictures, of course, can have a tremendous impact as the latest technology provides us with breathtaking images of the miracle of life before birth.

Sometimes people are shocked when they find out that a baby has a heartbeat at 20 days and all of its vital organs at 8 weeks. And often, when they see a life-sized model of a baby at 3 months, they are amazed.

With the facts before them, the couple need to ask themselves whether they're making an informed decision or looking for a quick fix to their problem. Are they thinking logically or running on emotions of fear and despair?

And because this is such an important decision, I urge couples to go and talk about it further. It's important to hear each other out, and it's also wise for them to include a third person so that they can get advice from someone who's not as emotionally involved as they are in the situation.

Seeking counseling before making such a critical decision gives their emotions a chance settle down and provides the opportunity to think more clearly.

Stay on Point

Sometimes a person will talk to you about a number of issues that are related to abortion or religion. Many times this is done to divert attention from the act of abortion.

The sidewalk counselor cannot allow himself to be distracted by issues surrounding abortion while the very act of abortion is being overlooked or even completely ignored.

You have to stay on topic and remind the person that they have a decision to make right now, and it's time to recognize that reality.

For example, when a person does not want the responsibility of raising a child they will come up with every possible scenario to justify the abortion.

Some common examples are: What if my baby is disabled, I cannot afford to raise a child, I am not ready to be a parent, and the excuses go on and on. These excuses are given to simply avoid any type of responsibility.

When somebody does this, they need to be reminded that they are already a parent and that the burden is not meant to be carried solely on their shoulders. They need to be reassured of all the help that is available to them.

And be careful not to get caught in the whirlwind of "winning an argument."

Unfortunately, winning an argument could very well mean that you lose the couple in the process. This is not the right time to be concerned about "being right." Rather, it's more important to win the hearts of the couple so that the goal – keeping their baby — is achieved.

Guiding them to the right decision by continually offering support in a loving manner is the best way to show them both hope and love.

Giving Space

And above all, respect the person's space.

We want the couple to know that we're simply offering help and hope. But, of course, it's their decision to choose to accept or decline that help.

That is very much in line with the teachings of Christ. Christ never forced anybody to love Him. Our Lord has always given us an open invitation. Jesus says, "Come and see ..." Yet, the choice is left entirely up to us.

Naturally, we pray earnestly that all these women turn around and choose to have their babies. It is absolutely heart breaking to watch them go through those doors of the abortion facility where they will be forever changed.

Still, it's necessary to respect their "space."

And psychologically that's the best approach to take. How do we react when we're approached by salesmen or people who are too pushy or forceful? We instinctively pull away or retreat.

And the same thing will happen outside the abortion facility. The people we want to reach will write us off. But if they sense we respect their space, they may be more willing to converse with us and be more open to receive help as well as the prolife message.

Sidewalk counseling is a delicate balancing act, which requires gentleness while conveying a strong sense of urgency. And it all must be done with respect.

When to Come – When to Go

The abortion mills where I've counseled usually open at 8 a.m. I would make sure to be there by 7:30. This is because the couples, understandably anxious about their decision, are often there early, waiting outside the door. This is a great opportunity for counseling as they wait silently in desperation.

Most of the time, I would counsel for approximately 3 hours before leaving. The nature of the task and the emotions involved can leave you depleted of energy after a few hours.

Who Likes Rejection?

Who likes rejection? Nobody! And constant rejections can be frustrating to say the least.

But when you decide to sidewalk counsel at an abortion facility, rejection is just a part of life. However, that's no reason to be discouraged. Counseling work is critical. The important thing to remember is to be a message of hope and love for these couples who so desperately need it.

And sometimes they do hear you.

One day a couple walked into the abortion facility unsure about their decision. An hour later they came out. I asked the man what happened, and he exclaimed, "We're keeping the baby! It is time for me to man-up!"

That response has stayed with me and given me hope. He admitted that it was time for him to take responsibility. He knew he had to take care of his "girl," and his little baby – to protect them from all harm. And when a woman receives such support from a man, she will find strength herself – the strength that dares to bring new life into the world, even in the face of adversity.

And we see in that strength the beauty of motherhood – and fatherhood. It's all about the couple and their baby – and that's the heart of the message we want to convey.

17 SIDEWALK COUNSELING
HARASSING OR HELPING

The atmosphere in front of an abortion mill can be surreal. Not surprising considering what is going on within its walls.

So for a sidewalk counselor to be able to function and not dissolve into a pool of tears, you have to put up a protective wall within. Remember, this is a spiritual battleground, and there is no time to be absorbed in "how I feel." These are the front lines!

The matter at hand demands two necessary ingredients: prayer and counseling. They are interdependent. All must be done in a spirit of deep humility, silence, and compassion, with the understanding that we are present for these troubled couples so that we can help them in their time of great need.

Unfortunately, they do not always perceive us as helpers.

When couples come to an abortion mill, they more than likely have spent a considerable amount of time and energy discussing their present situation. At this point, they just want to get this horrible experience over with. Their defenses are up, and they don't want to talk about the matter any further.

Raw emotions of fear and anxiety have overcome their reasoning. They will try to shun or silence any attempt to approach their problem logically. They have come to a dead end of despair. Even if there is hope they are not open to it because their "tunnel vision" refuses to allow any light in.

Sadly, they will perceive help as harassment. Of course, this is their guilty conscience talking, and, struggling with their guilt, they go into "attack" mode and accuse the counselors of harassing them, or else they ignore them altogether.

Recently, I had an experience at an abortion mill that illustrated this quite clearly.

A couple was looking for a parking space. I went up to the car to tell them where they could park. Of course, my plan was to give them literature on a pregnancy center that was down the road, which I did. The woman was very receptive and appreciative. The man driving the car remained silent.

They went to park their car and were gone for quite some time. Perhaps, they changed their mind? Well, not exactly.

Eventually, they came walking down the street to the abortion mill. Just before the man entered, we had a quick exchange. I offered him prolife literature, and he retorted by saying that I was harassing him.

I explained that we are only trying to help them. He said that I approached them while they were in their car assuming that they were going there for an abortion. Hence, it was harassment.

Well, first of all, I showed them where to park and simply offered (not forced) literature so that they could get help if they so decided.

Also, this facility's main income overwhelmingly comes from performing abortions. I reminded him of this, and as the door shut behind him, I also reminded him that the next day was Mother's Day.

If he was open to hope, he could have seen I only was trying to offer him help. His girlfriend was open to hope, but he was guarding her with an iron claw.

As people of "life" we must remain people of hope, who offer help at all costs – even in the face of accusations of harassment because these cries of anger or rage outside the abortion clinic are only the outward signs of guilt and great sadness for those who are on the verge of abandoning all hope.

18 ST. PATRICK'S DAY PARADE 2013

Honestly, I didn't know what to expect.

It was the first time I was going to march in a parade. And it wasn't just any parade. It was the annual St. Patrick's Day Parade, dear to my heart for a number of reasons.

First of all, I'd be celebrating my Irish heritage of which I am very proud, and I'd be honoring St. Patrick, my namesake. (My middle name is Patrick).

Also, I'd be representing the unborn, marching with the local right-to-life group. In a rather hostile, modern world, that was a challenge I was proud to take up.

But I did have some reservations. How would the onlookers react? Would there be hostility or confrontation?

When I arrived at our designated meeting place, it looked like we might be quite a small group. And as the minutes ticked by, I became increasingly concerned since there were not nearly enough people to carry our banners, flags, and signs.

But as the time for the parade to begin approached, our numbers started to grow. Soon we had 20+ joyful, spirit-filled, prolife marchers, eager to march as witnesses to life. I was excited but, even still, uncertain as to what to expect.

The parade finally stepped off, and the number of spectators was quite impressive. As we continued for the next hour and a half with periodic stops, there was something that made me think of another procession that took place some 2,000 years ago – the journey of the Lord on his way to be crucified.

Of course, I don't mean to imply that our parade was in any way comparable to the Passion of Our Lord in its significance. But, as we marched down the streets – watching the people who were watching us go by — I couldn't help but feel that this crowd, with its variety of responses, was probably not too different from the crowd that Jesus encountered so long ago.

Three reactions stood out.

Small groups along the way clapped and cheered for us and our cause. It took guts for these people to raise their voices and applaud amid the silence around them.

Perhaps there were others who were on our side but lacked the courage to speak out.

But those that did speak up reminded me of Veronica's encounter with Jesus on His way to the Cross. Out of sheer love and compassion, she consoled Our Lord by wiping His face.

Unconcerned about the thoughts of others, she acted without hesitation and without fear. Her love touched Our Lord so much that He left His facial imprint on the cloth. Veronica's courage was rewarded. The supporters of life exemplified this same type of courage, which is driven by love undaunted by fear.

The second reaction that I noticed was one of opposition. Honestly, this was the reaction that I was anticipating, and I had been pro-actively planning how I would react to it.

But to my surprise and delight, overt hostile behavior was nearly nonexistent. Only on a few occasions did I hear any comments.

But this also led me to think about Our Lord's Passion. The crucifixion of Our Lord took place largely due to the disdain a rather small number of people had for Him. Their hatred and evil motives spurred them on to brutally mistreat Him ... to the point of death. Is this not what the abortion industry is all about as well? The women are exploited as their babies are brutally led to their death. Only hatred and evil motives can do this! These are the very pillars of the abortion industry.

The third reaction of some of the crowd was actually not a reaction at all. It was their lack of a response that left an eerie cloud of stillness in the air. It made me wonder what was going on in their hearts. Were they being quietly polite? Were they afraid to speak up? Or my biggest fear — were they just completely indifferent?

This possibility of indifference scared me and left the biggest impression on me! Have we become a society so used to abortion that we're not even bothered by it anymore?

I'm afraid so many have become numb to the reality of what abortion is and how frequently it happens. Approximately 4,000 babies will lose their lives tomorrow in the United States alone. This will be repeated on a daily basis, unnoticed by most of us who live in the land of the free.

Likewise, while Our Lord's Passion was taking place, the vast multitude of people were indifferent. To many, it was just another day. Just another criminal being crucified for breaking the law.

Our Lord's dying in such a brutal way out of love for them and us certainly deserved so much more than such indifference. Likewise, doesn't the heart of a troubled mother warrant our attention? Doesn't the life of an unborn baby in jeopardy call for our attention? Can we afford to be lukewarm?

These reactions that I witnessed took me into the heart of Our Lord's Passion. And through the experience, I found a great gratitude for those who bravely support the unborn, the strength to pray for those who hate us, and a renewed vigor to educate those who just seem not to care.

As we continue to speak on behalf of the unborn and their mothers who are in such great need, let us ask Saint Patrick for his protection and guidance.

19 LIFE IS GOOD

In 1989, brothers Bert and John Jacobs began selling designer T-shirts out of an old van in the streets of Boston.

At first, they were not very successful. Then, one day they put a smiling stick figure on a shirt with the phrase "Life Is Good." Bingo! They sold 48 shirts in under an hour. That was only the beginning of their adventures that made their company an international success.

One day, my co-worker Jack – a good-natured guy with a sunny disposition — came into my classroom wearing a "Life Is Good" T-shirt. We started to joke around about the message on the shirt. But I noticed that whenever he wore it, it seemed to give rise to good feelings in us, and those around us. I think it subliminally made us aware of how much we had to be thankful for. Yes, it reminded us, life is very good!

But recently, I was thinking about another dimension of that simple, but profound phrase. And that is: All stages of life are good – filled with dignity and deserving of respect.

However, our society often finds it hard to see that. It seems more and more like a world where those in need are regarded as an inconvenience. Or, even more chilling, a world obsessed with removing all suffering, at any cost.

Take three groups where the frailty of human life is most apparent — the unborn, the disabled, and the elderly.

The Unborn
Since 1973, the unborn have been denied their most fundamental right — the right to life.

We do not want them, but we refuse to put them up for adoption. Somehow, that is just unthinkable. How is ending a baby's life even an alternative when adoption is acceptable and available? Finding a home where they can be wanted and loved — is that too much to ask?

The Disabled

Those that are disabled rely on all of us to be patient and caring. As a people of God we are called to love. Sometimes this love requires a great deal of sacrifice.

We find out quickly that real love isn't about flowers and a box of chocolates. Rather, it's about sticking it out when you only want to run away. It's about remaining silent when you want to scream. It's about giving one more time, when all you really want is to find some time for yourself.

God gives us the strength to love, and we need to implore Him for the gifts of patience and perseverance. If we answer the call to love without measure, those who are disabled can teach us lessons that we will carry with us for a lifetime.

The Elderly

The elderly offer us a lifetime of experience, full of wisdom to be treasured. But as they get older, frailties of mind and body become evident. Alzheimer's, Parkinson's, and dementia rob the elderly of their freedom. A broken hip can quickly sideline a person, which can rapidly lead to a permanent state of immobilization.

Yet, we have to remember that God is with us. Our Lord allowed Himself to be frail and vulnerable up until His very last breath. He did this so we may all have life and have it abundantly.

All throughout our lives we are challenged with suffering. Of course, nobody enjoys suffering but when we "walk through the fire," we can come out of it a better and stronger person. And this true for the elderly, too, as they undergo, perhaps, their last trials before they go to the Lord.

Obviously, we seek out to relieve the suffering of our loved ones. But it can be very difficult to bear with. And today, many have gone so far as to say, "If somebody is suffering greatly or severely disabled, just end their life. Why let them suffer needlessly?"

They say the elderly and the terminally ill should have the "right" to end their own lives, as an act of mercy, with the blessings of the state.

These proponents of euthanasia and physician-assisted suicide have lost sight of the true value of suffering.

As a people of life, we are called to be a people of hope. We are called to alleviate the pain of those who suffer by sharing in it. And this isn't easy, because we're human, and we want our loved one's pain to end. But by standing by their side with compassion in their time of need, we can bring them solace.

Mother Mary showed us this by her example as she remained with

Jesus to the end at the foot of the cross. Let us stay closely united to the elderly as they endure their sufferings.

The unborn, the disabled, and the elderly remind us of the frailty of life. They show us all how utterly dependent we are on God. The challenges that come our way are an opportunity for us to grow and an invitation to love during difficult times.

In this way, we will all see the beauty that can come out of suffering and realize that, even in these situations, "life is good."

20 "IT'S A WONDERFUL LIFE"

The movie "It's a Wonderful Life" is shown on TV every year, right around Christmas time.

The main character, George Bailey, played by Jimmy Stewart, is down on his luck, filled with despair, and on the verge of committing suicide. Bitterly, he tells his "guardian angel" he wishes he'd never been born.

The angel decides to grant him his wish. And he shows George what the world would have been like without him, if he never existed.

And through the alternate world the angel presents, George comes to realize how much he has impacted others by the love he has shown them – and how the lives of his loved ones, friends, and entire community would have been so sadly diminished if he hadn't been there.

Eventually, he begs his angel to give him his "old life" back. That's right, life with all its imperfections — even with his enormous debt, mean-spirited people attacking him, and the future looking bleak.

He craves to have it all back. For now, he sees the beauty of his family, his friends, — and it is a wonderful life, filled with love that he both freely gave and received.

Relating this movie to abortion leads one to think about the more than 56 million U.S. babies who were never born. What would their lives have been like? Who would they have become? What impact would their lives have had on the rest of us?

Sadly, we'll never know. One of those babies might have been the doctor to cure cancer. Another could have been a world leader that brought many countries closer to true peace. One could have been a servant to the poor and destitute in the world.

Unfortunately, we may have destroyed our future by destroying our youth. When we ask God, "How come you don't solve the many problems we have in the world?" He might just reply, "I sent you the solution. But you aborted that life!"

God calls us to love and be loved. This is the end result and all that really matters. George realized this when he got his "old life" back and found an abundance of love and support from his family and friends who truly cared about him.

Love is really the answer to all of our problems. It might sound too simple. But perhaps we too often overthink and complicate matters. Maybe we need to sacrifice a bit more and trust in God more as well. God tells us all things are possible, but that doesn't mean they're necessarily going to be easy.

Difficulties are part of life and we are called to hope, not despair. We're called to help one another. Deep down, I believe people are good, and they want to help those in need. You see this in dire situations when compassion brings great numbers of people forward to help in some way.

Perhaps we can extend that hope and love to women who are contemplating an abortion. Then they will realize, like George, that love and support are out there for them, as we lovingly show them that "Yes, it truly is a Wonderful Life!"

21 DOES GOD KNOW?

Year after year, as we gaze on the nativity scene at Christmas time, it fills us with joy and warmth.

We imagine how it must have been – the silent, holy night, the newborn King asleep in heavenly peace in the arms of his beautiful Mother. But is that the way it really was?

I don't think so. From what Scripture tells us, for Mary and Joseph the time surrounding the birth of their Son was tumultuous and filled with confusion, uncertainty, and danger.

It began when the Virgin Mary was told by the angel Gabriel that she was to bear the Son of God. The gospel tells of her great trepidation, and we can only imagine how she feared others would react to the news of her pregnancy — especially Joseph. And he was likely shocked and troubled, brooding over what had happened and what he was to do next.

Then, when it came time for Mary to give birth and she needed a place of warmth and safety, the young couple found there was no such haven for them. There was no room in the inn. And they had to manage as best they could among the dry hay and warm breath of the oxen in a cold cave nearby.

And later, after the birth of Jesus, Mary and Joseph, warned that Herod was seeking the death of the Christ Child, were forced to flee the country to save the life of their newborn son.

Before, during, and after the birth of Christ, the Holy Family was in distress, alone, and on the run. They had to face the doubt of others, rejection, and hatred.

And as I was contemplating this, it struck me. Isn't this exactly the situation of so many women today who find themselves unexpectedly pregnant?

Their personal "nativity story" seems very much like what the Holy

Family experienced: no place to go, the embarrassment of social stigma, not knowing what to do next.

And on top of that, add financial pressures, perhaps fear of being too young to cope, and the anger of unsupportive family members or friends who focus on the perceived inconvenience of the baby, and it's not hard to understand how a distressed woman might easily fall prey to those who say that abortion is the only answer.

Confronted head-on with adversity, she feels isolated. The walls close in and seem impenetrable, towering above with impending doom. There's no solution in sight. All seems hopeless.

She cries out to God, "Do you know? Do you understand what I'm going through? Do you know how I feel?"

Yes, He knows.

And not only does He know, but in the wondrous mystery of God made Man, He has seen such sorrow played out in His own life story. And He acts.

He came to troubled Joseph in a dream and gave him assurance and strength. Isn't that exactly what the expectant pregnant mother needs in her time of confusion ... assurance and strength?

He sent to Mary and Joseph the love of the three kings and the little shepherd boy who warmed their hearts in an otherwise cold world. Sometimes a woman needs a place to stay. Sometimes she needs a home. Most of all, she needs to know that people truly care about her.

And when the soldiers of Herod marched toward Bethlehem to take the life of their son, God led the young family to a place of refuge in Egypt, guiding them along a perilous journey to a place where the child could be safe. And that is what all parents desire — a place of stability, safety, and love where their child can grow.

Yes, God knows. And He will care for the frightened, pregnant woman just as he cared for Mary and Joseph. We need to encourage her to bring everything to God and trust Him explicitly, and He will show her how close He is during these times.

As we kneel in adoration before the Christmas manger, let us pray for all women who are preparing to bring their children into this world. May God send them good people to stand by them and help them in their need. Let them be surrounded by love.

"For unto us a Child is born, a Son is given."

ABOUT THE AUTHOR

Sean Patrick Miller

Sean has been active in the prolife movement since 1994. He has volunteered with Fr. Frank Pavone, the 40 Days for Life, and the Rockland Right to Life Committee. His contributions include sidewalk counseling and praying in the "public square," in order to positively send the prolife message to those in need. He is a guest blogger for the Rockland Right to Life website, RocklandRTL.org.

33077184R00038

Made in the USA
Middletown, DE
29 June 2016